The Essence of
Being a Woman

JANELLE SAAR

Balboa Press books may be ordered through booksellers or by contacting:

Balboa Press
A Division of Hay House
1663 Liberty Drive
Bloomington, IN 47403
www.balboapress.com
1 (877) 407-4847

ISBN: 978-1-4525-9309-8 (sc)
ISBN: 978-1-4525-9310-4 (e)

Library of Congress Control Number: 2014903260

Printed in the United States of America.

Balboa Press rev. date: 03/17/2014

BALBOA
PRESS
A DIVISION OF HAY HOUSE

Contents

Introduction

This book began as an inspiration to share everything I want my two nieces, Brittany and Taylor, to know about being a woman. What began as a gift to them turned into finding my divine assignment to inspire women to live in passion, power and purpose. Sometimes we find our greatest gifts in the most unlikely places!

The words contained in this book poured from me as I found my own essence embedded in the message I was sharing. It is my hope that these messages will call to your heart and vibrate your soul as they awaken the amazing woman inside you!

Deep in your heart your core essence is a sacred powerful space. My wish for you is that you find the magic and blessings in being you!

Find a comfortable place to get quiet and prepare to connect to that sacred powerful space inside you. As you read, I encourage you to listen for the messages your heart and soul are sending to you. You are an amazing woman and it's time for you to awaken to the power in your core essence! May this book take you on a journey to the essence of being a woman! It's time to discover who you really are at your core essence!

Be love

Love is the center of your entire being. You came here in pure unconditional love. As a woman, you were granted the privilege of receiving a girl heart that, by its very existence, implies it is overflowing with love. Love fuels everything that makes the world go around on this planet and throughout the entire universe. You hold the keys to an internal infinite source of pure divine love. Live your life fueled from that love within your heart. Live your life sharing your love. The source of love is infinite and the more you share, the more comes back to you!

Be the flow

A woman's essence flows like a river meandering through the countryside. Women are designed by the Divine to flow freely with the energy of life and emotions, without restrictions and obstacles. Life is full of all types of people and you will encounter those who say you are too emotional and too sensitive. A woman true to her heart and her essence knows there is no such thing. When your emotions are rooted in your truth and your power, they are exactly as they should be. Stay open and live your life flowing with divine source energy. Know that your gift of being a woman in flow allows you to connect from your core essence to anyone, anywhere in the world. Your flow has the ability to reach through time and space to places beyond this world!

Be you

You are always more than enough. The Universe created a perfect you with all your gifts and imperfections. In your core essence you have a knowing that connects you to your true self. In that space, you know exactly why you are here, who you are, your power and your purpose. You came to this planet with infinite potential, so be all you came here to be! When you forget or get disconnected from you, go to your heart. Your heart always knows your true core essence and your true north. Your heart will always remember and be your compass back to being you!

Live in your
sacred heart space

Inside you there is a sacred heart space, designed and created solely for you by the Divine. As a woman, this space is your anchor, your compass and your guide. Your heart always knows what is best and your heart always remembers who you really are. The Divine gave you the gift of your heart space as a reminder that you are the daughter of unconditional love. There is an infinite pool of divine love and light in your heart space. That infinite pool contains enough love and light to fuel the entire planet. You always have the gift to open your heart, live in and share this sacred space that is uniquely yours!

Own your vulnerability,
it is your power

Life will try to teach you to retreat from vulnerability. You will get hurt. After all, you are human and being vulnerable is part of the human experience. Your power as a woman lies in your ability to forgive yourself and others who have hurt you. Know there will be a possibility of hurt and stay open anyway. To be vulnerable is to know that risk exists and to give all of you, even though you know the risk. This is the only way to fully experience life. If you want to fully embrace all life has to offer, you must be willing to offer all of you. As a woman, you get the choice to heal the hurt and live fully, over and over in your lifetime. Own your vulnerability, choose to heal when you get hurt and embrace all that life has to offer you!

See beauty all
around you

The magic of the Universe is everywhere! You have the power to choose to live life as though every moment and every experience is magical! Your gift as a woman is to see magic and beauty all around you. Most people find beauty in the obvious. The gift of a real woman is to find beauty in those people and things where most only find flaws. As a woman, you are blessed to see beyond those flaws. Inside, you know the Universe makes no mistakes. Therefore, every flaw is a divine blessing and a sign of divine love. Seek out the magic of the Universe and find beauty in everything around you!

Live in connection

The souls of women thrive on the connections we create and participate in. You are always connected, so live in that space. When you face times in life that you feel alone, know it is only an illusion. Whatever you are facing, you are not alone! Ask for and search for a sisterhood that provides you with divine, out of this world, connections. You are always one breath away from living in connection. Our fuel comes from our togetherness so you have the ability to see the divine connection in every soul and every thing. Live your life as though you are connected to every person and every thing around you, because you are!

Treat your feminine body as a divine temple

Your feminine body gives you a contractual agreement with the Universe for creating life. Own that contractual agreement! Whether you choose to create life or not, own the power you possess to make human life. The feminine body is the reason all human life comes to this planet. The feminine organs are the life line of all humanity. They are the generator that fuels all of mankind. You have the power to create the magic of life from your body, so treat your body as the divine sacred space that it is!

Feel all your emotions,
every single one of them

As a woman, you are designed to feel all your emotions: the good, the bad and the ugly. It will be tempting at times to turn off your emotions so you do not feel the bad and the ugly. Please know it is impossible to turn off the bad and ugly emotions without also turning off the good ones. To have the great emotional highs that life is all about, you must be willing to feel your way through the bad and ugly emotions fully open. Know when you are open, you will find your way through the tough times. This is where you will experience the great emotional highs because you had the courage to face the emotions on the other side!

Always be light

Life will have ups and downs, good times and what appear to be not so good times. Know that every experience you have here on this planet serves a purpose. There are no coincidences and no accidents, only divine orchestration. When life delivers you times that appear not so good, look for and ask for the lessons. Know the lessons are here to expand you, to grow you and make you more. We grow most dynamically outside our comfort zones, so embrace the gifts that lie there. Inside you there is always light; connect there when you are in a growth cycle that challenges your current being to be more. Be light even in the darkness!

Find your divine
assignment

You came here with an amazing purpose that the Universe selected as the perfect divine assignment for you. It is a purpose that aligns precisely with your unique gifts. You are the one and only woman to fulfill this assignment. At times you may feel disconnected from what you are truly here to do and you may feel ill equipped to own your purpose. When this happens, be still with yourself and look deep inside your heart. In your heart space, you will find your divine assignment, exactly what you are here to do, and the strength to own both. You already have everything inside you that you require to fulfill your divine assignment. Believe in yourself and own what you are here to do. When you awake to your divine assignment, you will move mountains. You are that powerful! The world awaits the unique gifts that only you can offer!

Live in abundance

Know that true wealth is so much more than money and material possessions. Wealth is living a life filled with happiness, joy, love, fulfillment and passion. There may be moments when you feel less than wealthy. In those moments, live in your heart and mind as though the flow of abundance is on its way to you. It is never far away. You are meant to have every single thing your heart desires. It is your birth right to live a life overflowing with happiness, joy, love, fulfillment, passion and money beyond your wildest imagination!

Play & have fun

There will be times when life gets heavy and you are overwhelmed with all that is happening. In those moments, take the time to focus on the lighter side of life. You are here to have fun and enjoy adventure! Explore the many opportunities that life presents to you to play and have fun. Learn what makes your heart overflow with passion and what fuels your soul, and then make those opportunities a priority in your life. Create the space for play! You were born to sparkle! Life is a dance and taking the time to play is the key to experiencing the entire dance. You deserve to play, experience adventure, laugh and have as much fun as possible in your lifetime. Choose to be you, have fun and live your sparkle!

Believe in
legendary & epic love

As a woman, you are entitled to be in a relationship that is so incredible it rocks heaven and earth. Be patient and wait as long as you must to find the person who creates love that rocks heaven and earth with you. You are too enormous to settle for comfort and safety. Own who you are! Find someone you trust with every ounce of your heart and soul. Someone who makes you more every day, someone who fills your heart beyond anything you believed possible before you met them. Find the partner who treats you like a queen. And when you find this person, be prepared to give them your heart and soul in exchange for their heart and soul. In this space of fully giving all of you, is where legendary and epic love is created!

Live in gratitude

Many people believe gratitude is an emotion.
Gratitude is so much more than just an emotion;
it's a lifestyle. A woman living true to who she is
knows that happiness does not bring gratitude,
gratitude brings happiness. No matter what
is happening in your life, you have the power
to choose to find gratitude in your journey
and the blessings around you. When you
choose to live a life of gratitude, you have the
ability to always find something or someone
to be grateful for. In the moments when you
struggle to find gratitude, look inside yourself
and be grateful that you get to be you!

Lead with invitation

Leading as a woman is about more than demanding that people follow you. Chances are you will play many leadership roles in this lifetime. Being a leader is being a mom, a wife or girlfriend, a business person, a neighbor and a friend, just to name a few. Life will give you many chances to lead. Women leading in their feminine power know they must first lead themselves by being true to who they are. A true leader knows her core and lives her life connected to the truth that lies there. Women leading in their feminine energy possess the ability to lead by inviting others. They know how to connect others with the best of what lies inside them. Find your gift as a woman leader to inspire and awaken passion in others!

Be still & remember

Life will get crazy and pull you in a million different directions. No matter how crazy the craziness gets, don't forget time for you. As a woman, you are many things to many people. The most important is being you for you. If you don't take the time to stay connected to your inner self, you and the many people in your life will suffer. Create quiet time to explore the inner depths of you and celebrate all that you find there. Take the time to slow down and smell the roses. Be still and remember you. In the stillness, you recharge and reconnect to your inner self!

Live each moment &
be present in the now

You create your own reality. As a child of the Divine, you have the ability to manifest anything you wish to create. So dream big, because fulfilling your biggest most audacious dreams is what you are here to experience. The past is behind you; bring only the lessons you learned from it with you to the present. You cannot live in the past. The future is a blank canvas and you get to paint your life's masterpiece. Visualize your masterpiece just the way you want it with every detail in place. Then live in the here and now as the person in that masterpiece. Embrace every moment with your full attention and your full heart. Be grateful for every single moment you are alive and every experience you have. In the end, your life is measured by the moments you are present in the here and now, truly living!

In Power Sisterhood's mission is to empower women by awakening them to who they are at their core essence. In Power Sisterhood delivers a message of love, inspiring women to live overflowing with an abundance of passion, power, purpose love, joy, happiness, gratitude, fulfillment and everything their heart desires.

The belief at In Power Sisterhood is that it is every woman's birthright to live an amazing miraculous life! In Power Sisterhood has created a growing community of more than 100,000 women aspiring to live their amazing miraculous life while creating connections with sisters around the world.

In Power Sisterhood inspires women awaken to their passion, power and purpose through daily inspirations, meditations, online webinars and workshops.

To join our sisterhood and learn more about

In Power Sisterhood products visit:

www.inpowersisterhood.com

www.facebook.com/InPowerSisterhood

Hearts on Hands

Hearts on Hands began in Denver, Colorado as an inspiration during a class certifying life coaches. The inspiration grew into a global movement. The mission is simple: transform your life by focusing on the power of love, light, hope and positive energy. Then transform the world by giving the inspiration forward to others.

Here is how the movement works. Draw a heart on the hand you do not write with. Every time you notice the heart throughout the day, feel the love, light, hope and positive energy around you. Then give that feeling and the message forward by drawing a heart on two other people's hands.

Making a difference in the world starts with one person choosing to do one small act. A simple act of drawing a small heart on your hand will infuse the power of love, light, hope and positive energy into your life and others'!

To learn more about the Hearts on Hands movement and to receive daily inspirations of love, light, hope and positive energy visit:

www.heartsonhands.com

Printed in the United States
by Baker & Taylor Publisher Services